Best Friends

Janan Jennifer Platt

DEDICATION

To Dragon, Cocoa, Telamia (previously the cat named "Bleu"), Eidon, Majid, and Aslam.

And not to forget, the squirrels, birds, trees and places that flew to be our family.

ACKNOWLEDGMENTS

This sweet story was not written by me,
Janan Jennifer Platt.
Rather, it was told to me.
It was a conversation, one day, with Bleu, now
called Telamia, looking at me,
as he shared the higher and deeper realities.
And it was the birds, the trees,
and all the animals.
Even the waves of the air conversed,
speaking of truths in limitless love and
boundless energies.

1.

I'm so lucky my kitties have each other

                                        We look:
                                        Eidon on
                                        The rock
                                        Hunting under
                                        The junipers
                                        Cocoa here,

patient
To play with and be with
Brothers & Sister—big family
Bleu: Best Friends.
Me: We're so lucky to live with our best friends
Bleu: like roommates,...
        We remember Horse, the big, grey cat &
orange cat, his brother
        The orange cat, he was nice
Me: I don't remember his name.
        (thinking, trying to remember...)
Bleu: Billy
Me: Buddy? Billy?
Bleu: Billy

2.

Me: Yes
        They were your friends. Do you miss
them?
        Concerned: were they your best friends?
Bleu: shakes his head 'no'
Me: Dragon. Dragon is your best friend.
Bleu: nods confirmation. Yes, Dragon.
        Skies & The All Allelueia
                Alleleuia
Bleu: Dragon.
Me: Dragon.
        Happy, Loving feelings.
        Remember how they played, chased,
        Tumbled, slept together,
        Were kind & concerned, and fun

3.

I write this story
        Bleu sits, waiting
We come to the part about Dragon
Chimes ring and ring and ring.
I finish the story, feeling the happiness
Bleu's head is lifted, listening
        Smiling. Birds twitter, arriving calling
I write this part
        Then get terribly sad—afraid
        Of losing him, our Dragon.
        Tears, little girl feeling
        Rosita—Little girl sad. Bereft.

4.

Bleu—afraid
Me—afraid
        Are you afraid?
        Am I afraid?
        Where is Dragon?

The elephant
        The elephant—45 years old, beautiful
        And loving
        Was killed his tusks and face taken
        Left like a dead mouse when
        Seen from outer space
    Sadness
Where is Dragon?
Bleu nods, settling into the chair on the lawn

5.

Me: "Dragon! Dragon!" I call

   Peace
     Air clears
      Water fountain peaceful, consistent
       Phil's garage is open
        Safe Haven
   Air smells wet cool, plants with sweet
         and mint
    When I turn my head that direction
  No thoughts between here, over lawns,
     to that garage – clean, clear
    unimpeded
  Bells ring.
        Birds call by the lake and I can hear them
           Doves near coo—gutteral & thick

6.

Bleu is on his chair now, he licking his
        Fur, smoothing it
      Such sweet smells
          Water, Flowers Earth
      "Shade Plants" Majid had said
          perhaps the mint.
I leap up from my chair, around the
    Front bend down to them.
      Sun on the crinkly leaves
        A shiver and quiver enlivens them.
Who would like to come?
          I ask
Not the ones in the sun
      not the ones in front
              Stillness.

7.

I look.
a fly on one
  Further back – tall mint
I pluck the tips
  Chimes ring one ding in confirmation
I plunk it in my lemon honey water
 lift the cup–
    So pretty. Mint Florette.
    Perfect.
Take a Sip.

8.

Meowing, Cocoa comes
  Bird in his mouth—limp
        Orange breast
    Baby Robin
  Went
Gone? I confirm
  Don't jump up and try to save it, him, it...
Cocoa growls, hiding behind the tall
  Juniper tree near me
 Drops his prey
I check again. No movement
  went.

9.

young bird
I am sorry.
I never meant to unleash the cats
    to kill anyone.

Cocoa is a loving way to go, though.
 He perches aside
Then pounces again, playing with the bird
But no life is left in it
 Bored, Cocoa comes and sits
   licks his paws.
"You must eat it," I tell him
      "You cannot just kill just to kill.
      You must eat your breakfast."

10.

Unconvinced, Cocoa plops on his side,
    Majestic, on the cement.
        Content.
Birds twitter
  They have come.
   "Cocoa," one says.
I look up, search the branches
  Over head==the large locust==
Are you Robins?
 The family members?
    come to witness?
To be with him

11.

That baby
 in death
sirens
  slow sirens
   low wail
  on the streets behind us
chirps
 a dove
twitters
 breeze
 chimes
 wind

12.

Now Dragon
 Slithers up, as if coming from the
 Ground before us
Where did you come from?
 I'd ask
 but I'm writing this
 and just happy to see him
 lots of chimes and birds and
    warmth of the sun
Firecrackers even—to the East of us
 it's only 9 AM
  on a weekend!

13.

That's my Dragon!
 As he licks the coconut milk from
 The bowl on the ground.
Then prowls to the fountain
 Pansy, The sunlight in stripes
  on his stripes on dappled water
   and rocks and dirt
   The jungle comes up
   we can taste it
   As he bends
    and takes a sip.

14.

Alleleuia is wonder—says the traffic far away
        Wonderful? Wondrous!
              I wonder not to finish it

  We look around: Cocoa, Me, Dragon
Where is Eidon?
  Bleu turns his head
The Robin—baby Robin chest up
     wings spread
        gone. Went.
Birds cover us
      in calls and chirps

15.

I'd call it
   Celebration
If it weren't for human conditioning
   Sentiments
 Release fat breath
  What feeling is this?
I didn't mention
That Dragon Cat
   Is bone and skin.
  Gone is his fat, plumpness.
 wasting away
  kidneys worked,
   too much stress,
      Bless Them.

16.

I hope for a miracle
every moment
please save him
Restore him
my precious one
my Beloved
my Dragon.

Amen

17.

I sit, for a while,
 like a cat
and watch
 and feel
 and listen
Birds now spread
 Someone clucks
A dove soars across the air, further
 Are you telling them?
 I ask – Beware, Cocoa is on the hunt?
Of course the birds
 can call him,
 name him,

18.

Cocoa lives among them
    among all of us

Cocoa, you must not hunt—
    I consider telling him
Before I lapse into
        Catness.

Majid and Aslam, inside
    are quiet,
Though I am sure
    are near the window
watching this

19.

waiting for mom—me—to get up
  come in
and take them
 to the world
  making the shift
  from cat relaxation
  peaceful soup of sounds and scents
to a jubilant stage coach wild mission
  But not just yet.
Butterflies are visiting us.
  Eidon has returned
    Cocoa is about to get a moth
      Dragon and Bleu are deep in relaxation.
                        We're all together
again in this love.

Amen.

ABOUT THE AUTHOR

Janan Jennifer Platt lived in a large house with a large yard, with her four cats and two dogs. They had fun every day. They took walks together down the street, with the dogs on leashes beside her and the cats running everywhere, up trees, and down trees, across the street, under the bushes, and finally, to their home.

They played in the yard, and played in the house. Where the cats were, the birds came. Dragon told Janan to throw food to the squirrels, so she did, mostly below the huge locust tree on the front lawn.

That tree showed shadows of its branches in the glow from the light over their mailbox at night. They had painted a mural on the walls of the living room, and so it looked like birds from the mural were flying through those shadow branches.

They were all very fond of each other. They
petted and played and ate really well. Janan
cooked for the animals, or just served the food
as fresh as she could. The house was always full
of rich smells: dinner cooking, or flowers from
the yard, or the smells of happiness and being
together.

In their times together, they made a lot of art—
paintings, big and little, vibrant and filled with
loving stories and revelations about everything's
soul. They made beautiful jewelry that made
people light up. They made movies! Of their
family and of yoga and comedies and funny
things about the experience of being human.

www.JananCreativeArts.com

They made two art galleries and sold a lot of
their art and a lot of their jewelry. They also sold
the wonderful art of fifty local artists! They held
events, created many spectacular email
newsletters, and raised money for charities.

www.JananGallery.com

And they wrote. They wrote, and wrote and
wrote and wrote.... They wrote so much that
they started a publishing company.

That company is Gorilla Publishing. It is mostly
stories and art and music and films from their
lives together and their observations and
experiences in the world, with contributions
from everyone and everything all the time.

www.GorillaPublishing.net

Their first book they published, and favorite
one, is called The Joy of Dog. It features Aslam,
the wonderdog, and all of them. It is a story that
they told together, including the keyboard of the
computer!

www.TheJoyofDog.com

Since they had been writing for years, they had
more books to publish. One was a script for a
movie, that they converted to a novel.

This is a great and funny book, called,
Will Rhypen: Couples Counselor.
It's is a comedy about love,
and has made many people laugh.
But it is beautiful too, with wonderful
descriptions of Nature. That's their specialty—
letting Nature describe Herself and speak
through them and putting it into print for
people to remember.

www.WillRhypen.com

Their beautiful new book,
Something So Magnificent.
has stories, recipes and poems
from the Animal Family.
Reading it, you will cook up a lot of goodness
in your life, and in your heart!

www.SomethingSoMagnificent.com

With Gorilla Publishing, Janan and her family
will publish 30 childrens' books,
20 memoir novels, 10 inspirational card decks,
art books, art products,
podcasts, music, games, and movies.

The movies they made include
short film comedies:

Mr. Boffo's Holiday,
Mr. Taken Dentity,
Takin' it to the Streets,
Adventures in Dumpster Diving,
This is Not Television,
and Yoga Mela.

And, of course, they have animal family movies!

www.JananFilms.com

The animals and Janan also gardened a lot.
They planted twenty trees, twenty rose bushes,
many lilacs, honeysuckles, and hundreds of
perennials.

Their yard was bursting with life!   It sang.
But many people in their neighborhood were
using toxic chemicals and poisoning the air and
water and life.

So Janan and her animal family created the
Applewood Sustainable Gardens Tour,
to help nourish beautiful yards in healthy ways.

www.GardensTour.com

For fun, and to give people gifts, they made
wonderful wineglass ornaments.
Eidon Cat made many pictures
with the wineglass ornaments.

www.WineGlassOrnaments.com

They have games, cards, podcasts,
art books, and inventions coming too.
There's lots of good in the world coming!

In all love,
Janan and her Animal Family

www.ingramcontent.com/pod-product-compliance
Lightning Source LLC
Chambersburg PA
CBHW081324250726
48662CB00008B/2742